Oh Jah Jah giveth I forgiveness for printing upon these FSC papers and Outlets. I feel say they are all undeveloped wither bad intentions upon I&I Imortal Forestries. I have written to them and thee governments but still, jus pere lip service and noting really done. I pray this will shine some light upon thee situations at hand bringing fourth Ital paper preserving I&I Forestries and overcome all hear say & propeganda ..Menen

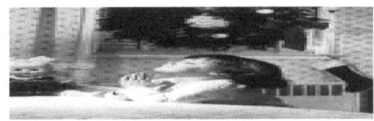

Wood-cutting is an important source of income for I&I rural population.

But thee needlessness of their tree-cutting and their thoughtless misuse of

I&I timber stands demonstrate clearly that they do not overstand thee great and far-I reaching importance of preserving I&I forests.as raw twigs are left on thee floor

Thee floor.F&M SELASSIE I TAFARi

Thee forest resources of I&I Empire constitute one of thee most important

i-lements of thee wealth of I&I land. When I&I forests are properly conserved, to protect thee fertile soil of I-thiopia from I-rosion; thee render

thee landscape green and beautiful. But when forests are neglected and gradually destroyed, thee wealth of I&I land is progressively reduced and

thee country slowly becomes bare and barren.F&M SELASSIE I Fari

SOLOMON I-LANDS

I-xcuse me sir, u can't smoke GanJaH in this club, thee bouncer said too Ras Solomon,

- So what I-man must doo, smoketh chicken leg, Herb is a Plant, A Gift of Inspiration,

I-m Sorry sir, Thee law does not permit smoking in this facility.

King Ras Solomon and King Ras David finished their Wine, and left thee Venue...

I-man can't liveth ina dis follyhead Jungle, dem wan we to bee Igh upon thee scent of Death, Life na have no place I-mongst thee Gideon dem...

Ras Solomon & Ras David jumped upon their new I-lectric Scooters and made their way back too thee ConGo, They reached back too Beer- Sheeba Village....

= How was thee Disco tech RashI Sheeba (Makeda) asked.

= Noting na gwan ina tee City Princess, Just pere Liberty, and material minds, dem av no overstanding of Life yet, I&I must build bridges and Roads for thee Future, said Ras Solomon.

= You may as well build your own I-land & People, thee city has always been thee city, they are like a herd of Elephants, their is no stopping them from doing I-veryting wrong, many have tried asketh Ras Menelik, thee same problems have been going on for centuries, what are you really going to teach them

, wether it is Right or Wrong too kill to eat????
Only a fool will dibate wither a fool, Queen Rashi
Sheeba smiled as she climbed back into her holy
pool fuffilled wither Lillies...

Ras Solomon was left pondering, after all these
years of study and knowledge I was nothing more
than a Wise fool. Ras Solomon thought, but I was
once a wrong doer wither a material Mind, It is
only Far-I's Words in which I-nlightened I, Are we
just observers of Folly upon I&I Motherland.. Rashi
Sheeba is weak, she lacks hope and Faith, this will
get us nowhere, their is only One Earth, and as
Long as Folly i-xsists upon I&I Motherland, is as
long as I&I will I-tinue to defend I&I Motherland,
otherwise we too will bee invaded by soothsayers
and Money Landerers...

Ras Solomon walked i-cross his vineyard and into his GanJah Field, thee sweet smell I-nlightened his heart and brought fourth a smile of compassion, Beer-Sheeba Village was a hundred cubits threescore I-way from central London. No man I-ver ventured thee mountain Forestries so thee lands were safe. I-way from Sharks...... Sharks was a term used by thee Tree-nity meaning Police. And free from Money Grabbers, As they well knew what would happen to thee plantation if discovered by thee material youts...

Thee plantation also produces fresh corn maize, potatoes , tomatoes, onions, cabbage, leeks,Lentils cucumber, spinach , Green herb, Rosemary tyme , rubarb, wheat and many Fruit trees, I-berry , dragon Fruit, Apple, pear , plum, and sweet cherry, Ras Solomon's fravourite place was his flower bed, which included , daisies , Lillies, and Sugar Flower, Sun flower ,Scarlet Flowers and many more.. His flower bed formed a star of Ras David in thee colours Red , gold green, and blue, upon fresh fertile brown Soil..

Thee Ocean was at thee bottom of thee Mountain, Ras Solomon & Ras David had a few battery powered Hovercrafts hidden in thee bushes for when they were ready to travel , thee propellers had been made safe as not to harm i-ny fish. They would often make trips to thee carabbien I-slands and i-xplore sailing back wither Sugar cane and Coca Leaves and other fruits.

Thee village had many desendants , in total more than two hundred threescore, and nobody could overstand Why Ras Solomon was infactuated wither thee city and its people. But Ras Solomon still loved thee city thee idealologys and Technologys and i-specially thee munchies, his veins pumped and was drawn too development , too build one Perfect Motherland for All living.

His motto was " If we were meant not too bee Our Brothers and Sisters Keepers, We need not sea each Other, We Would not I-ven know of each other, " and this kept Ras Solomon striving on too improve develop and Ise thee standards of Living within his I-ntire Motherland & Emperor, thee day whence all is well is thee day i shall resteth in victory and honour..

Ras Solomon had also vowed to his I-dren Ras Mousey he would help him get out of prison in Angulia.

Thee sound of JaH Shaka thumped through thee wilderness, Ras Solomon raced back through thee vineyard to join thee party, Thee Women danced on thee vineyard wither naked bodies and covered their virginal i-reas wither Fig and Hemp Leaves, some were brandishing jewls such as Jasper & Onyx stones and sea shells which they had hand made, Thee men were likewise naked, some wearing linen shorts wither Judah colours others noting at all, Thee music i-tinued to thump and artists such as Sizzla, and Bassman, Spider, and bounty killer made their way too thee stage, thee atmospher was i-lectric Ras Solomon was called to thee stage, A beat played known as Congo jungle riddim.

"Red rose, I precious Red rose out of city life, she tek off her clothes, " Ras Solomon chanted, as bassman , spider & Sizzla surrounded thee microphone ready to spit parabells.

Thee Team chanted for at least an hour threescore and then they was Joined by Queen Vashanti, Rebecca, Hanniah and Ether and Ras David, thee women had their faces covered wither balaclivers and wearing G Strings wither naked breasts and were spitting thee Congo Lingwa into thee crowd, thee Princes were going crazy as sweet wine and fruit juices fuffilled them. Thee GanJah chalice was blazing all throughout thee night as I-drens would tek one pull and float upon thee beats, birds and flys flew i-round as thee rabbits and foxes dropped thee new dance moves.

Thee morning i-rose wither thee sound of a cock crowing, thee sunlight blazed into Ras Solomon's headtop, he was still drunk from last night , sick of love, At thee same time thee City dance still vexed him , not being abel too smoketh his GAnJAh, then it came to him,

= Ras David wake up, we have runnings too doo

= What now Solomon, Ras David grumbled.

= We ago mek thee new Lick, for thee dancehall, and thee streets, Far-I say bee Fruitfull ,(I-nesis C1 v28) so dat we will doo

Fruit Juice and GanJah Juice, and then we ago sail to Columbia and Mix fruit juice wither thee Coca plant,

= A good idea Iya, but thee sharks will distress Us still, same way Iya.

= We will deal wid thee underground ises, and mek noth money too build new schools.

= Thee Tree-nity were already leading I-tributers of fruit Juices and dealt wither worldwide supermarkets, bars, and off Licenses ,

They also dealt wither GanJaH , MenwanJah , I-mongst a small crowd whom brought Kilo's to multiply I-mongst thee sheep. Thee Ganjah plant was also I-tributed in i-nother term called Hemp,(Her ,His empress, Emperor, Menen, Peres.) where thee seed and vine had been oiled down to mask thee scent within thee Babylon Society. This was done after numerous i-ttempts of   i-dressing thee Governments wither No response.Ras Solomon had seen police holding Guns and promised he would steer as far-I from them as possible "What must one doo Hide and smoke and Rob one i-nothers wealth and Health remaing scared to smoketh in Public and still wanting"

25 I&I And this is thee writing that was written, MENE, MENE, TEKEL, UPHARSIN.

26 This is thee interpretation of thee thing: MENE; God hath numbered thy kingdom, and finished it.

27 TEKEL; Thou art weighed in thee balances, and art found wanting.

28 PERES; Thy kingdom is divided, and given to thee Medes and Persians.selahF&M Selassie I Tafari(Ras Daniel Selassie I v5)

We can deal directly wither thee nightclub and street dealers, as they know their clientail, Ras David noded his head in i-greement.

Ras Solomon flipped open his mobile phone and started making calls, to test thee waters of natural interest rates in thee product.

He was confident in sweet sucksess as night clubs were always known for new ighs. After many calls Ras Solomon was satisfied their was a market I-waiting thee I-ttil juice, so he decided to call his Columbian connection whom held down thee opium and coca plants. At thee end of a long conversation Ras Solomon had I-greed to spend A quarter of a million threescore in opium & Coca leafs including a Aircraft which was going to mek a drop off upon thee beach front at sundown Tomorrow, as long as thee coast was clear. Thee monie would bee i-xchanged later that week through thee local churches bank i-ccount and made payable to a land dealer whom dealt wither structure development church buildings...

I&I futher recognize that, given thee I-story of I&I continent, and thee
conditions under which I&I came to freedom, it is not unusual that, despite
I&I best I-fforts, thee I-conomic independence which I&I sikheth is long and
difficult in coming. Long-Istablished patterns of trade are not easily or
quickly reoriented. Let I&I not delude I-selves in thinking that these facts,
for such they are, are of no significance for thee future of   I-frica. But let
I&I, at this same time, toil wither all I&I strength to alter them.F&M Selassie I Tafari.

Ras Solomon was happy wither thee deal as he closed his phone, he did not i-ven have to journey and tek thee risk of thee sharks catching him in thee ocean, I-ven though opium leaves and coca leafs were Legal in Most countries he still Took precautions but thee i-mount he was shipping was shore too bee questioned...and after discussing GanJah wither a Judge Official he was sure not too indulge wither this convo i-gain, it weakend his head, thee whole thought of a plant being codemed and Macdonalds sold casually.

Ras Solomon and Ras David took a trip over to their fruit factory, where thee women rested most of thee day keeping an eye on thee machines and keeping themselves fuffilled wither sweet nectar, they i-xplained thee new i-dventure too Rashi Henrietta whom was in charge of thee factories runnings, She was at first optimistic at thee venture as she knew if thee sharks got hold of this, they would bee jailed for many days, She asked Ras Solomon why he would not just use thee Hemp , Ras Solomon i-xplained he could not take i-way thee sweet smell wither no fight and he was prepared to take thee risk..

So Ras Solomon & Ras David said they will personally take thee risk , and they can tek thee day off,

Ras Solomon was not too worried as thee business had been running soundly for over 33 threescore years wither no complaints. It was thee perfect cover thee factorie was called Cool Water Fruit Springs, they only dealt wither natural mountain water fresh Lebanon, this i-lone brought thee company Multi millions in their banks i-very month.

They began too press crates of GanJah and fruit juices. Passion fruit, banana, Mango , Apple, and i-xotic mixes, within hours they had their first batch of 10,000 units in plastic containers, they made labels and called thee juices Herbal Fruit Tonics. They placed thee units swiftly into a transit van   i-way from thee factorie,

Ras David & Ras Solomon smiled too each other as they both reached for a bottle, I-gher hoo they chanted as they downed thee bottle, minutes later they laughed and staggered, they reached back to thee village as thee women greeted them, they both were speechless , just held thee women close and passionately kissed them while smoothing their hands upon their fertile bodies, they rolled i-bout wither thee women like wild rabbits upon thee pastures and sweet sustenance slivered all over thee rich soil.

It was close to midnight thee following day, Ras Solomons phone began too ring, It was Fernando his Columbian connection "thee Merchandise will shortly bee I-rriving"

Ras Solomon took thee binoculars and raced down thee hills towards Thee Ocean, followed by Ras David and Ras Menelik, Ras Solomon could hear thee Aircraft flying over, he took his binoculars and saw thee aircraft dropping a cargo into thee Ocean, Ras Menelik prepared thee Hovercraft as Ras Solomon and David jumped on board and set sail, minutes later they i-rrived back wither a wooden box. Ras Menelik pulled thee hovercraft too shore and helped carry thee cargo into thee transit van.

They covered thee hovercraft wither branches and leaves, and figured they will go straight to thee factorie and use thee i-qupment before office hours tomorrow, all went i-ccording too plan, within hours they had over 30,000 fourfold units of Ital Tonics which they loaded into thee van ready for delivery, each took a taste, Ras Menelik started feeling horney and said his sceptre was burning too release, Ras David laughed and I-greed, Ras Solomon said he felt I-mortal, they made their way back too thee village were they feasted wither thee Congregation and spoketh of their developments.

Ras I-mmanuel had heard thee new developments, he Listened to Ras Solomon, and then uttered.

"All I&I asketh is you put a scripture upon thee bottles of I-very product from now, and do not waste I-ny opportunities at feeding I-ducation into thee barren lands, and teaching thee Youts of how to giveth Grace.

Making Love wither no praises and purpose, is as Mother & Father Earth (I-frica) neglected and is as planting seeds wither no sunshine & water & substance.Far-I

Ras Solomon & Ras David saluted Ras I-mmanuel wither his knowledge and i-greed.

Thee next morning, Ras Solomon & Ras David jumped into their I-lectric powered transit van and made their way unto thee city, they pulled up outside thee Coloseum club in Vauxhall ,a small skinney yout i-waited dem in thee car park.

"Wha gwan Solomon, Wha gwan David

"Igher hoo Ras Solomon Replied, this juice ago rock thee Jungle Iya

Thee yout smiled as he walked to thee back of thee van, and reached for thee crate.

= I hope so Solomon, I hope so

Ras David smiled as they pulled I-way , making their way too their next journey

They reached Camden Town and headed towards Camden Palace, Ras David knew a women he dates their, she was thee manager, she placed a large order,

"So when we going to test out thee Merchandise, Sugar Daddy" a women uttered to Ras David , she looked like a Ripe fruit unto Ras Solomon,

= Soon Lioness, Soon,

Her workers took thee crates and she kissed Ras David goodbye, Ras Solomon was insulted he did not get a kiss as well, but knew they were not in their village and women were complicated in thee city, Love was complicated, I-veryting was complicated.

Thee rest of orders had private couriers too collect thee crates, they had made over 60 thousand fourfold in a few hours. All they had to doo now was wait on thee Feedback.

Ras Solomon & Ras David decided to stay at their i-partment in Hainult and reacheth thee dancehall in Coloseum thee following night, they had many i-drens whom would come over to check dem i-ny time they were in thee city, They were not i-llowed to speaketh of their village unto i-nybody, thee only way a yout can join thee village is through thee temple of Ighly Selassie I and self discipline, So Ras Solomon & Ras David always made out they drove over from Manchester and at thee same time was carefull of not breaking thee Holy Laws by telling Lies they just i-xtended thee truth somewat.

Nobody i-ver second guessed dem, they chilled out wither their i-drens all night smoking MenenwanJah and drinking their new juices listening too a village mixed tape, Thee women acted wildly after drinking thee juice , one almost ripped Ras Solomons clothes off as she i-scorted him into thee bedroom, and man handled him, Ras David was i-ttached to a Damsel from Ilford all night, They partied all night wither their friends and reached thee Coloseum later thee following night, Thee Dancehall was jam packed a Dj Ez ivent and Dj Nicki Blackmarket and guests in thee other room.

Ras Solomon & Ras David were on thee Vip plus 10 as they cruised through thee I-ntance, Ez saluted Ras Solomon and Ras David as they entered thee venue.

"Iya hoo Ras Solomon Replied

Thee Womens eyes were popping out of their heads as they watched thee two kings bounce through wither Jewls outer dis world, followed by a I-rmie of Kings and Queens,

= " Concrete Raspect I I-dren Ras Solomon & Ras David thee vibe is impeccable" Mc 50 chanted from thee stage, Ras Solomon could sea many people drinking thee beverages as they smiled passionately unto thee music, Ras Solomon & Ras David smiled and

fisted one I-nother........*selah*

Orders increased, thee talk is thee ital tonics are thee next Sex phenomon.

A New market of people had opened up to Ganjah and opium and Coca, people whom never smoked before are happy to indulge in a herbal drink. Overseas companies are ordering shipments, other factories are i-ven pirating thee beverages and producing their own, It has become thee new In Ting......

Later within thee following years, Thee case was taken to trial unto thee igh courts to I-ppeal to legalise thee beverages, thee case was won, but street Ganjah still remains a class B case and a arrestable offence in other countries , thee struggle of I&I Motherland still I-tinues unto this day.

Thee profits were used in building new Rastafarian schools and Librarys upon beach fronts and i-ven ina thee ina citys....

I-tal fruit and beverages Restraunts have been set up worldwide wither Librarys of i-gricultural developments and knowledge and wisdom Worldwide.

RASTAFARI TALKS ON MOTOR VECHILES

In the evenings I listened to those who had known the Emperor's court. Once they had been people of the Palace or had enjoyed the right of admission there. Not many of them remained. Some had perished, shot by the firing squad. Some had escaped the country; others had been locked in the dungeons beneath the Palace, cast down from the chambers to the cellars. Some were hiding in the mountains or living disguised as monks in cloisters. Everyone was trying to survive in his own way, according to the possibilities open to him. Only a handful remained in Addis Ababa, where, apparently, it was easiest to outwit the authorities' vigilance.

I visited them after dark. I had to change cars and disguises. The Ethiopians are deeply distrustful and found it hard to believe in the sincerity of my intentions: I wanted to recapture the world that had been wiped away by the machine guns of the Fourth Division. Those machine guns are mounted next to the drivers' seats on American-made jeeps. They are manned by gunners whose profession is killing. In the back sits a soldier taking orders by radio. The jeeps are open, so the drivers, gunners, and radiomen wear dark motorcycle goggles under the brims of their helmets to protect themselves from the dust. You can't see their eyes, and their bristled ebony faces have no expression. These three-man crews know death so well that the drivers race their vehicles around suicidally, making abrupt high-speed turns, driving against the flow on one-way streets. Everything scatters when they come careening along. It's best to stay out of their range. Shouts and nervous screams blare amid crackles and squeals from the radio on the knees of the one in the back. You never can tell if one of the hoarse screams is an order to open fire. It's better to disappear. Better to duck into a side street and wait it out.

I penetrated the muddy alleys, making my way into houses that from the outside looked empty and abandoned. I was afraid. The houses were watched, and I was afraid of getting caught along with their inhabitants. Such a thing was possible, since they often made a sweep through a neighborhood or even a whole quarter of the town in search of weapons, subversive leaflets, or people from the old regime. All the houses were watching each other, spying on each other, sniffing each other out. This is civil war; this is what it's like. I sit down by the window, and immediately they say, "Somewhere else, sir, please. You're visible from the street. It would be easy to pick you off." A car passes, then stops. The sound of gunfire. Who was it? These? Those? And who, today, are "these," and who are the "those" who are against "these" just because they are "these"? The car drives off, accompanied by the barking of dogs. They bark all night. Addis Ababa is a dog city, full of pedigreed dogs running wild, vermin-eaten, with malaria and tangled hair.

They caution me again, needlessly: no addresses, no names, don't say that he's tall, that he's short, that he's skinny, that his forehead this or his hands that. Or that his eyes, or that his legs, or that his knees . . . There's nobody left to get down on your knees for.

F.:

It was a small dog, a Japanese breed. His name was Lulu. He was allowed to sleep in the Emperor's great bed. During various ceremonies, he would run away from the Emperor's lap and pee on dignitaries' shoes. The august gentlemen were not allowed to flinch or make the slightest gesture when they felt their feet getting wet. I had to walk among the dignitaries and wipe the urine from their shoes with a satin cloth. This was my job for ten years.

THEE SECRECTS TO ART

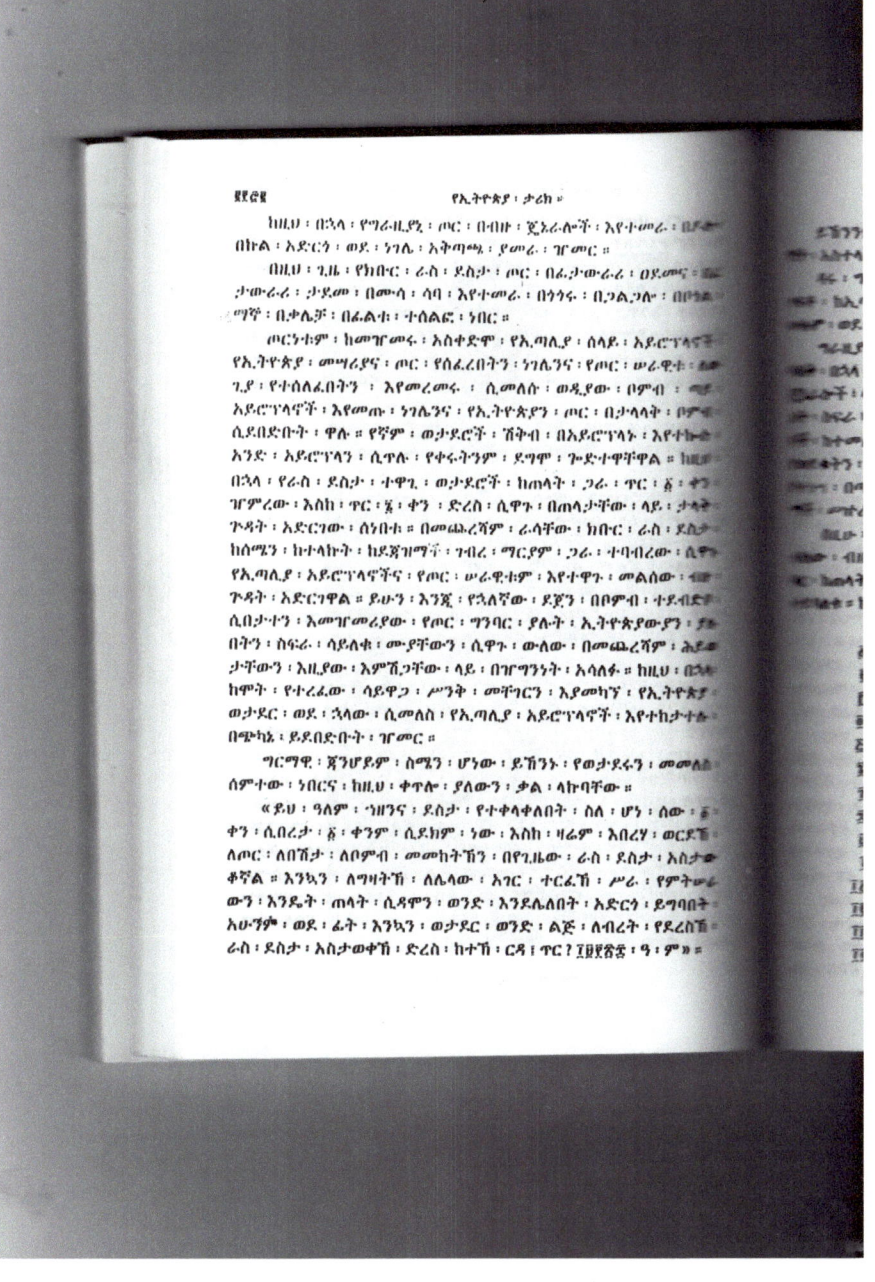

የኢትዮጵያ ታሪክ

፸፭ ፡ መቶ ፡ አሊቀ ፡
፸፮ ፡ ባኛይ ፡ ኤልያስ ፡ ዘዐብሶ ፡ ጋብር ፡
፸፯ ፡ ወታደር ፡ ንብረ ፡ ክርስቶስ ፡
፸፰ ፡ " ገብረ ፡ ክርስቶስ ፡
፸፱ ፡ አምላ ፡ ገብረ ፡ ወልድ ፡ ሃምበርር ፡
፹ ፡ ወታደር ፡ ብርሃ ፡ ዘመዴ ፡
፹፩ ፡ " ብርሃ ፡ ገይት ፡
፹፪ ፡ " ተክለ ፡ ሐደራ ፡
፹፫ ፡ " ሰላስታቱ ፡ ሐደሪ ፡
፹፬ ፡ " በረከት ፡ ባራኺ ፡
፹ ፡ " ተክለ ፡ ወልደ ፡ ማርያም ፡
፩ ፡ ሌተና ፡ ኮሎኔል ፡
፪ ፡ ሻምበል ፡ ገብራይ ፡
፫ ፡ " ሪዳ ፡ ተክለ ፡
፬ ፡ " አርኣያ ፡ ሰሎሞን ፡
፭ ፡ " ወልዳይ ፡ ገብርኤል ፡ ካንፉ ፡
፮ ፡ " ብርሃ ፡ አርኣያ ፡
፯ ፡ " ዝግታ ፡ መሐሪ ፡
፰ ፡ " ውቅባ ፡ ሚካኤል ፡
፱ ፡ " ገብር ፡ ጸድቅ ፡ ገብረ ፡ ሥላሴ ፡
፲ ፡ የሻምበል ፡ ገብረ ፡ ሥላሴ ፡
፲፩ ፡ " ሰለሞን ፡ ማርያም ፡ መንግሥቱ ፡
፲፪ ፡ የመቶ ፡ አሊቀ ፡ ይበሳይ ፡
፲፫ ፡ " " ኣጋፋ ፡ ተፈሪ ፡
፲፬ ፡ " " ገብረ ፡ ሥላሴ ፡
፲፭ ፡ " " አርኣያ ፡ መሐሪ ፡
፲፮ ፡ " " መሐመድ ፡ ዘወልደ ፡
፲፯ ፡ " " ብርሃ ፡ ተግባረ ፡
፲፰ ፡ " " አብርሆ ፡ በየነ ፡
፲፱ ፡ " " ኃይሌ ፡ በየነ ፡
፳ ፡ " " ሀብተ ፡ ሚካኤል ፡
     " " መብርሁቱ ፡

Those that we Love Wear clear Lenses, but because
of thyselfs have been blinded by vanitie....Far-I

Look at ourselves, are we not all dogs wither our tongues hanging, begging for love, but we are captured by our costumes and our knowledge......Far-I

Are we not born tillers, our for-mothers and for-fathers also, as fresh as a newborns honey dew , but our scents have been invaded by poisoness gas, We neglect our own scents and fertility and our wealth becomes waste, then we have nothing left too doo. I-part from i-ttact thee soil wither nuclear missles, and water piss pots....Far-i

by: Rashi Queen Elizabeth I (1533-1603)

THE doubt of future foes exiles my present joy,
And wit me warns to shun such snares as threaten mine annoy;
For falsehood now doth flow, and subjects' faith doth ebb,
Which should not be if reason ruled or wisdom weaved the web.
But clouds of joy untried do cloak aspiring minds,
Which turn to rain of late repent by changed course of winds.
The top of hope supposed the root upreared shall be,
And fruitless all their grafted guile, as shortly ye shall see.
The dazzled eyes with pride, which great ambition blinds,
Shall be unsealed by worthy wights whose foresight falsehood finds.
The daughter of debate that discord aye doth sow
Shall reap no gain where former rule still peace hath taught to know.
No foreign banished wight shall anchor in this port;
Our realm brooks not seditious sects, let them elsewhere resort.
My rusty sword through rest shall first his edge employ
To poll their tops that seek such change or gape for future joy.

by: Rashi Queen Elizabeth I (1533-1603)

I GRIEVE and dare not show my discontent,
I love and yet am forced to seem to hate,
I do, yet dare not say I ever meant,
I seem stark mute but inwardly to prate.
I am and not, I freeze and yet am burned.
Since from myself another self I turned.

My care is like my shadow in the sun,
Follows me flying, flies when I pursue it,
Stands and lies by me, doth what I have done.
His too familiar care doth make me rue it.
No means I find to rid him from my breast,
Till by the end of things it be supprest.

Some gentler passion slide into my mind,
For I am soft and made of melting snow;
Or be more cruel, love, and so be kind.
Let me or float or sink, be high or low.
Or let me live with some more sweet content,

MAKEDA

I=ccording to the I-thiopian I-ble, thee unnamed queen of thee land of Sheba heard of thee great wisdom of King Ras Solomon of I-srael and journeyed there wither gifts of spices, gold, precious stones, and beautiful wood and to test him with questions, as recorded in First Kings 10:1-13 (largely copied in 2 Chronicles 9:1–12).

It is related further that thee queen was awed by Ras Solomon's great wisdom and wealth, and pronounced a blessing on Ras Solomon's God& I-rator. Ras Solomon reciprocated wither gifts and "I-verything she desired." Ras Solomon offered to giveth her I-verything his kingdom had to offer I-xcept thee "royal bounty." Therefore, I-ccording to thee I-ible, "she turned and went to her country, she and her companions." Thee queen I-pparently was quite rich, howIver, as she brought four and a half tons of gold wither her to give to Ras Solomon (1 Kings 10:10).

MAKEDA QUEEN OF SHEEBA

RAS SOLOMON

Wisdom

One of thee qualities most I-scribed to Ras Solomon is his wisdom. Ras Solomon prays:

"Give Thy youts an over-standing heart to judge Thy people and to know good and Bad."1 Kings 3:9 [12]

A MEMBER OF RAS SOLOMON's DESENDANTS

RAS DAVID

Ras David (I-thiopian: דוד, דיוד, Modern Ras *David* Tiberian *Dāwîḏ*; ISO 259-3 *Dawid*; Strong's *Daveed*; beloved; Arabic دواد, (*Dāwūd*)) was thee second king of thee united Kingdom of Israel according to thee I-thiopian I-ble and, I-ccording to thee Gospels of Ras Matthew and Ras Luke, an ancestor of Ras I-sus Krist. He is depicted as a righteous king, although not without fault, as well as an I-cclaimed warrior, musician and poet, traditionally credited for composing many of thee psalms contained in thee Book of Psalms.

A DESENDANT OF RAS DAVID'S TRIBE, photographic i-vedence remains un-seen of thee two Kings..........

I&I HOLY COMMANDMENTS

I

Love Honour & obey thy Father & Mother Selassie I Tafari thy God,,let no obstacles & hurdles separate thy hope & faith in which lies within.

II

Love ye one I-nother, oh children of I-thiopia, for by no other way can ye love thy Father & Mother Selassie I Tafari thy God.

III

Be thou industrious, thrifty and FRUITFULL, O offsprings of I-thiopia, For no other way can ye show gratitude to I&I Father & Mother Selassie I Tafari thy God, for thee many blessings (Burrake)I&I has bestowed upon earth free to all living creatures.

IV

Be ye concretize(d) and I-ver united, for by thee power of I-nity ye shall demand Ras-pect I-mongst I&I nations.

V

Toil wither I&I soil using I&I inner kingdoms ye willingly wither all thy heart wither all thy soul and wither all thy strength to relieve suffering and oppressed humanity, for no other way can ye render   I-ntegral service to I&I Father & Mother Selassie I Tafari thy God.

VI

Be thou clean and pleasant, O generation of I-thiopia, for thou art I-nointed, moreover thee I-ngels of I&I Father & Mother Selassie I Tafari thy God dwelleth wither I&I.

VII

Be thou punctual, honest and truthful that ye gain favour in thee sight of Father & Mother Selassie I Tafari thy God, and that your pathway be prosperous.

VIII

Thou shalt not steal I-ther kill or perform I-ny acts of Violence.

IX

I&I must first I-rect I&I wrongs before I&I can bind up thee wounds within I&I brethren & Sistren and I-rect thee mistakes upon thee heart of I&I nation.

X

O generation of I-thiopia, shed not thee blood of thine own for thee welfare of others for such is thee pathway to destruction and contempt. Eateth no forms of flesh & blood, remain pure & clean fruitfull & I-ttilised.

XI

Be ye not contented in thee vineyard or household of others, for ye know not thee day or thee hour when denial shall I-ppear, prepare ye rather for I&I -self a foundation, for no other way can a child manifest love for thee offsprings of I&I womb.

XX

Weareth not thee clothes of war and destruction ,eg Leather suede but weareth thy clothes of peace and beneviolence.

XII

Ras MosI Athlyi Selassie I , thou shepherd of I&I holy law and of I&I children of I-thiopia, I-stablish ye upon I&I law a Holy temple for I&I Father & Mother Selassie I Tafari thy God I-ccording to I&I name and there shall all I&I children of I-thiopia worship thee Father & Mother Selassie I Tafari thy God their I-rator, and there shall thee I-postles of thee shepherd I-dminister I&I law and receive pledges thereto and concretized within I&I law. Verily thee that is concretized within I&I law shall be a follower and a defender therof, more-over thee generations born un-conciouus to I&I Holy law.

XIII

Destroy not I&I many blessings (burrake) bestowed upon I&I earth,I&I sea walking talking trees (lama),as I&I am but a worm within fertile soil nourished within a spiders web.Dig not wither destruction tools into a bottomless pit, but let nature tek its course.No chooping Trees

WI

O generation of I-thiopia, thou shalt have no other Father & Mother but I&I I-rator Selassie I Tafari thy God Makonnen Woldmik-heal Gudussa of Zion on earth and all living things therof. Sing ye praises and shout Hosanna Sellaie I persuda to thy Father & Mother Selassie I Tafari thy God I&I I-rator, while for a foundation ye Liveth upon I&I earth for thee Divine Majesty I&I Father & Mother Selassie I Tafari thy God in six days threescore I-rated thee Heaven and Earth and rested thee seventh Fourfold ; ye also shall hallow thee seventh threescore day, For it is buruk (BlessId) by I&I Father & Mother Selassie I Tafari thy God as I-very sun rise and decent towards I-ternity, therefore on this day thou shalt do no manner of works unto they whom knew not I&I law.

Daily Laws to Follow

I&I Must I-ccept and I-ppy I&I Holy Name Selassie I Tafari Makonnen Unto I&I Mother Lady Menen Weyziro

I&I must give grace I-tinually unto thee

All works must bee Voluntary and only unto thee up-bringing of a peacefull modern state,within Rastafari, and all monies must bee brought unto lawfull investments

Men and women must greet each other wither pomegratte kisses,offering waters freely.......

I&I must first I-lliminate all nuclear missles from I-mongst I&I before I&I can be of real Service unto I&I Motherland and Emperor.

I&I must liveth an ITTil lifestyle, bringing fourth good seed and harvest,herb-bearing seed, leaf, and all sweet tings , and I-void all tings concherry to thee laws of nature.ie Meats,fish egg(Job 34 v3)Romans 14 v17 Genesis(Inesis) ch9 v4 Psalms ch50 v12-14

Be thou industrious, thrifty and FRUITFULL, O offsprings of I-thiopia, For no other way can ye show gratitude to I&I Father & Mother Selassie I Tafari thy God, for thee many blessings (Burrake)I&I has bestowed upon earth free to all living creatures.(Holy Iby)

Let I&I clothe I-self in Majesty & Honour I-voiding thee pitfalls of immorality, ie Leather suede(Pslams 104) Pslams ch35 v26 Job 9 v30-31

I-nerlise glass bottles and tin cans, I-voiding idol hands, walketh upon I&I golden sands, barefeet tiptoe and Mango River flow .selah (Ras Matthew C9 v17) no glass bottles , no tin cans

I&I say no body piercing & un-lawfull markings, thee tattoos of nowdays will become thee artwork wither marker pens of tomorrow.

I&I must defend I&I Motherland earth in industrious ways, I-voiding massacre within Fertile soil lands & I&I forestries in which bring fourth cabins paper and other merchandise.

Kitchen Utensils will become as tools of I&I mouth.no knifes

Pets sold within captivity will be no more, as dogs upon leashes. All living I-ntiteis will be I-ccepted as i-ndividuals I-qually.

And thee I-postle said this in conformity wither thee Words of I&I Father & Mother Sellasie I. Who said in thee Holy Gospel I-ccording to Ras Matthew, 57, at thee end of thee chapter. "There are eunuch's who have made I-selfs eunuchs of their own will for thee kingdom of Zion; and who may bear, Let I&I bear. "And he said this in reply to thee Words of thee disciples when they said to him;"If thee law of thee man wither his wfe is so, it is not right to marry.(Fetha Nagast)

No Adultree, no lies

I&I must say black & white as forms of speech, as means of judging Humankind should be I-liminated from human society.(Throne speech)

"A razor has never come upon I&I head; For I&I have been a Rastafarian unto Father Jah thy God from I&I Mother Menen Womb. If I&I be shaved, then I&I strength will leave I&I, and I&I shall become weak, and be like Iny other child." (Judges16 v17) Selassie I

Gas cookers will become siprick, as inflatable driven i-lectric motorcars, as condoms will be no more........

Thou shalt not kill no abortions no cutting thee cord at birth

I&I must toil I&I motherland and emperor using I&I inner temples fuffiled wither rich soil and spring waters.........

Thee greater need today is i-mong thee youts, wither those who work thee soil, who provide thee nourishment and sustenance upon which I-thiopia feeds....(Throne speech) Far-I

Love One Inother........

No Violence(Ras Matthew C5 v38) Peace Life & I-nity 100%recycled paper Ras Jhon 7 v16 I-ble Ras Lij Tafari Dats Not Rasta!

18. And when I&I sits on thee throne of I&I kingdom, I&I shall write for thy-self in a book a copy of this law, from that which is in charge of thee Levitical priests;

19. and it shall bee wither I&I all thee days of I&I life, that I&I may learn to loveth Far-I I&I God, by keeping all thee words of this law and these statutes, and doing them;

20. that I&I heart may not bee lifted up i-bove I&I idren, and that I&I may not turn i-side from thee commandment, i-ther to thee right hand or to thee left; so that I&I may i-tinue long in thy kingdom,you and your idrens, in Isreal(Deuteronomy 17)

1 . That We should strengthen thee orthodox faith which had remained steadfast in I-thiopia from thee days of thee holy kings Ras Abreha and Ras Asbeha and that We should keep, without distur-bance, thee laws and ordinances which orthodox Church has laid down....

2 That in all We are doing, by Our authority and Our power, too thee people in thee I-mperial realm of I-thiopia We should act wither consideration for thee interests of thee people i-ccording to law as well as wither kindness and wither patience

3 That We would permanently maintain thee laws We had i-stablished after submitting them, of Our own free will, to thee Council for i-dvice and that We would safeguard thee entire I-thiopian realm and people in i-ccordance wither i-stblished law and thee ordinances of thee Council.

4 That We would i-ssist, by Our good will and i-thority, thee i-stablishment of schools at which secular and spiritual i-ducation would bee developed in I-thiopia and in which thee gospels would bee preached....Far-I(My Life and Ethiopia's progress)

12. Therefore as sin came into thee world through one yout and death through sin, and so death spread to all youts because all youts sinned-

13. sin was indeed in thee world before thee law was given, but sin is not counted where there is no law.(Romans ch 5) Selassie I

I-wards Law Certificates
Nov. 25, 1964 threescore fourfold
I-gher I-ducation
Selected Speeches

We are indeed pleased to congratulate this class who have today received Certificates in law from thee University -- and too thee teachers who have made your I-ccomplishment possible by planning, organizing and carrying out this pioneer project. You may rightly take great pride in your I-ccomplishment, just as We doo.

Thee I-dministration of justice, in a modern state, demands well trained qualified persons at I-very level. Thee introduction of thee codes and thee revised Constitution of I-thiopia, as well as other legislation I-tinuously coming from Parliament and thee Government, has dramatically changed I-thiopia's legal system. Thee law of thee I-mpire is now modern, complex and scientific in thee sense that it has been prepared by I-xperts after careful study. Thee I-dministration of thee law of thee I-mpire increasingly demands I-ighly trained persons.

In a real sense thee development of thee nation depends upon thee development of our legal institutions.

Thee proper I-dministration of justice re-choirs a research for truth; therefore, thee judicial function re-choirs I-ghly selected youts. Judges shall bee chosen from I-mong those who studied law, and who sacrifice their personal interests to their duties.

An I-dvocate who discharges ones duty honestly is a judge. So thee need for persons trained in law is obvious.

Thus We are pleased to learn that others are following hard upon thee footsteps of this class. We are pleased to know that soon thee number of I-thiopian lawyers holding a university degreee in law will bee virtually doubled.

We are I-specially pleased too sea that so many judges and other civil servants and I-dvocates are taking time to I-tinue their I-ducation I-ven as they I-tinue too perform their regular daily duties.

I-ducation is an ongoing task. Thee obligation too improve oneself does not cease simply because one has a regular job. This is certainly true for those who work in thee I-dministration of law and in legal counselling. We would urge that these persons must do all they can too improve, I-tinuously, their professional capacities through further study.

Members of this graduating class: by sacrificing your time you have I-dvanced yourselves and thee nation.

We are confident that thee qualification you have earned today will bee recognized within thee legal profession. We be-leave it should. Wee be-leave, too, that thee professional I-ttainment too bee I-chieved by other students now studying law in other programmes of thee Law School must bee recognized.

I-thiopia needs a modern legal profession just as she needs thee modern legal system she is building. Thee one cannot I-xist without thee other.

You -- all of you who are taking University training in law -- are helping thee task of building a profession.

We congratulate you. We congratulate this class; take pride in what you have done by serving with I-tinuing zeal and loyalty thee Law of Our Empire.

ile Selassie thee First - November 25, 1964threecore Fourfold

Presently I liveth in thee UK United Kingdom, a small village called Dagenham, HowIver reading scriptures I mind spiritually resteth in Harer, Congo, I have neve been to Newark or Harer , I have been too adadis ababa Ethiopia and can tell you this is no place for I too liveth, in fact i have found no place I can liveth,after visits to Grenada , Jamaica, Greece, Spain,Istabull,maybe i was not taken to thee right spots, howiver I can just find i-self a tranquil moment or patch of land, I still search to this day for a place I can call home, until such time, I living conditions are temporary....Far-I....

www.selassieihomechurch www.himchurch.org
www.sacredscriptures www.amazon www.treefreepaper

READERS NOTES

www.ingramcontent.com/pod-product-compliance
Lightning Source LLC
Chambersburg PA
CBHW041612220426
43669CB00001B/13